"The only way to be truly free is to be informed and seek equality, not only for yourself but for your brothers and sisters."Thank you to all who've supported me and continue to do so, and thank you for supporting the practice of being an informed individual.

A special thanks to Mr. Russel Castro. We are the universe, discovering the universe, to inform the universe about itself.-Chopra

The following pieces are double spaced in order to leave room for the reader to annotate and leave notes for themselves.

enjoy.

Family

A bond held by at least two loving individuals is family; no need for any blood bonds or marriage proposals. If you so love an individual (and both consent to the title) then it is as claimed. If this is so, then why do we put limitations on that statement? Who are we to say that there are limitations? We are but equals and fellow citizens who have no more say than any other, nor any less. So if two may love each other who is to say they can or cannot start a family with children? Why does the role of parents have to be held by a man and woman? Why are these predetermined rules in place? Are we not all equals? Are we not all under the same flag? Do we not follow the same laws and rules? If so, then why are some punished and told they are not as free as you and I? Discrimination of any form is immoral and wrong if done without just cause, and little to no discrimination has just cause. We all lease the same land and drink the same water and till the same earth, so why are we treated so differently? Why do we fight so hard to keep each other down instead of elevate each other? We're all brothers and sisters so why do we so hate our brothers and sisters? We must make the choice to love, not hate, and end the discrimination and prosecution of others. If one so desires to begin a family, why does it matter the gender or sexual orientation of that one?

Fight

Why should the men and women of America be forced to fight in unjust fights that do little more than line the pockets of the top one percentage? In 1775, we fought, bled, and cried for a nation we would design to be an international harbinger of freedom and liberty, in 1940, we sent our boys across oceans to fight for what was truly right and to protect not only our nation but the world. 1861, a nation divided fought itself, brother against brother causing a self made holocaust in a show of true humanity and mortality. Other than these examples, all battles ending with American bloodshed were for nothing more than government and corporate greed. Not to belittle casualties involved in other wars, for every American death is one to be mourned, and every American soldier is one to be honored. But why should our sons and daughters be forced to fight in an unjust war? If no just cause presents itself in the case that the well-being of our own or another justice seeking nation is at risk, then thc foreseeable sacrifice of our nation's populous should not be a question. Every man, woman, and child's life is of equal value, and one should not be forced to offer his or her life for a cause that is not just. I understand the necessity of a draft in times of dire need, but in a nation where the military is larger than any other and there's no direct threat to life, why should we force any citizen to relinquish his or her rights as an American? We should be willing to fight for a nation that we live within and advantages we surely use, but we should not blindly follow to our deaths. If the need for action is in question, then why should action be used alone for force in a fight that no one wants to take part in other than the corporate owners who run our lives?

Healthcare

A universal healthcare system will do more good for this nation than one could imagine. We're the only first world nation without a state based healthcare system. How can we claim to be the best nation and a nation that is truly free when others lives are valued more highly? Why is the woman with three children, two jobs, and no husband's life worth less than the young man's who has just graduated from Harvard law and has a top end job offer right out of school? Despite what challenges we've faced and what choices we've made, we're all human beings, and we are all equals. Some of us have had terrible struggles and pains throughout life, and those of us who have still deserve a right to life and the right to a healthy one. There are those who truly cannot afford to feed their families, to keep their homes, and still have enough to insure their lives and we as a nation of freedom and acceptance should truly be accepting and help our brothers and sisters in need. If we take insurance out of taxpayer dollars, the cost of insurance will show little to no change in price and will now include all citizens. Even if your workplace claims to provide insurance, you're still paying for that out of pocket just, as of now, it is indirect, if it is taken out of taxes, you will now receive that extra money in direct pay instead of insurance, and with this, we will all have equal healthcare instead of having to pay thousands for decent health providers. With this comes not only doctor's visits, but also all pharmaceuticals and surgeries. This will work to also start the breaking down of the pillars of corporation beginning with the pharmaceutical companies, and it will work to take the trillions out of the corporations pockets and place it into the masses.

Ignorance

Intolerance and a lack of compassion has led to a state of ignorance in the nation we call home. We point fingers at each other, creating marginalized groups who we claim to be equal, but we treat as lessers. The minority groups in our nation have long felt oppression at the hands of their brothers and sisters due to the corporate influence that hangs above and falls down upon us in a constant state of crushing weight. The corporate overlords prey on us like mice and put us against one another like wild animals all for their material gains with no care if we live or die and no care if we're starving in the street with no place to lie our heads. If these titans of industry that we feed every hour of our lives and every dollar in our pockets to don't care about us, then why do we worship them like gods? Ignorance is the answer. We're too focused on publicity and tabloid articles and buying that new toy we kill ourselves over.

We're too focused on hating and scratching and fighting to realize the atrocities happening right in front of us. We're blind to the damages happening to our society because of our own selfish gains . We're so trained to love and worship the business world, we lost sight of our humanity. We're ignorant to the real world and live in a fantasy that the lords of the land have so carefully constructed for our fragile minds in order to brainwash us to their agenda. We must snap out of this constant mindset of fantasy and realize the truth in order to tear down these walls and flood in with the masses to end the constant suffering that plagues us.

Mendacity and Mediocrity

Deception has long plagued our once great nation in not only the political scene, but also in news media. We sit day to day, divided by the constant discourse of our nations so called leaders, allowing them to sweep us into the endless rabbit hole of "he said she said" nonsense that only seems to grow our president's and other figure head's twitter following. And from this, who is really to blame? The American public, the very people who this child's play harms the most. We sit on our sofas and watch the news, popcorn and sodas in hand, drooling over the next outrageous thing President Trump posts and how we will gossip about it with our colleagues, saying how much of a terror he is and how smart we believe we are. Well, if that's true, then why do we allow our nation to fall to these painful lows? Why do we allow the mediocrity of Trump's rhetoric to stain our ears? Why do we allow the mendacity of politicians who say they care about us, but then stab us and the working man in the back once we vote them in? Why don't we stand up against what is wrong in this nation and unite as a people with common goals and form a unity and bond that our founding fathers once held? I challenge you to stand against the hate and dishonesty placed upon us. I say to no longer let the media and the politicians divide us. Black, white, gay, straight, and every person in between stand together to fight for not only yourselves, but your fellow brothers and sisters. Stand side by side against the corporations who wish to divide us and pave the way for a new, bright future for every generation that comes after us and hope for a day that our children and our children's children no longer have to experience the hate that still fills this nation's heart. Together we can make a nation worth fighting for and a nation that I would be proud to belong to. Go out and inform your neighbors and friends; don't let them believe lies like "my vote doesn't matter" and "there's nothing I can do, I'm only one person", because every vote matters and it's our duty not only to ourselves, but to our nation to shape the political scene how we see fit. _Every person can make a difference. Whether it be from leading rallies to walking in marches or even as simple as clicking that cast ballot button in the booth, every person matters and is needed. Let us fight together for an expanded workforce, let us unionize ourselves for the rights to a livable wage and a healthcare system available to each and every one of us. Stand together to help others and pass laws to help the low income family with a father and mother working two jobs each that still can't support their family. Let us push for an increase in funding to education so the next generation may be more informed than the last. Let us stand together to fight for our rights not only as americans, but as human beings. The inequality that has for so long scared the people must be brought to an end, but this can only be achieved if we stand together a nation united.

Public education

The current public education system can be defined as mediocre at best and at worst an absolute abomination. An entirely revamped system is well overdue in American education. Every day, there are technological and social advances, yet our classrooms stay the same. Low funding to small schools, subjects well outdated, and a majority of teachers who've seemed to have lost their drive. The next generation is suffering, we fall further and further behind in the scholarly race and our children less and less prepared for higher education and that's if they even decide to go. We see the low test scores and, instead of thinking a new way to teach or getting in the classrooms and helping, we decide to instead just pass the children through on things such as alternative graduation plans. They claim these routes are for the children who aren't college focused - a polite way of saying they didn't care enough to educate our children. Aside from the few that are truly gifted and the few with disabilities, children's minds, for the most part, are similar to one another and it is the school system's job to educate and drive these young minds to better things. But, when we have undereducated teachers and others who simply don't care, the children suffer. Now this isn't to say that there aren't teachers who do care and who do try hard, but I've met many more on the opposing side. I come from a high school that offers two graduate tracks :tops Tech. and tops University, the former of which prepares students for the work force and the latter for some form of higher education, but I will say both are jokes. Tops Tech is a medley of electives such as home ec. and welding, while tops University is classes that are required by University for entry but, unless you're in the honors, gifted, or advanced placement sections of tops University, you basically only have blow off classes that do little more than just pass you through. Once you graduate, you're either ill prepared for college (and in all likelihood will drop out) or you're prepared only for the workforce but were never taught about workers rights and how you should expect to be treated or where to find a job so you're severely exploited by your employer. I say do away with the duel track and focus on getting one track right before expanding, set higher goals for your teachers, and penalize the ones who truly don't seem to care. Encourage students to attend a secondary school and don't let them just set their goals at making money, but rather making a difference. Fuel the next generation to be better than ours and any before it and the one after them even more so. Don't settle for mediocrity, make something of yourself and help your children do the same. We must raise funding to public school systems so that they have access to better teachers and equipment, along with a more advanced work environment. Don't let the politicians say that public education gets enough funding, because it doesn't; I promise you that. My junior year of high school, all of my classes were in trailers. If public education funding is so high, then why was that the case? Why is it that education is the first to be cut? Is it not one of, if not the single most, important things in our nation? Help the next generation achieve greatness and fight these atrocities.

Stand together

We must help one another to prosper in this brutal reality of a world. We hold too much of a reliance on the monetary value of items; this reliance causes the discrimination of our brothers and sisters who come from lower standings in society. Why should something such as water be processed, sold, and held to a point of accessibility only to those who can afford it? We don't choose the situation we're born into, so why should we be punished and penalized for it? The one who yells get a job to the one who begs for money is an ulcer on our humanity. What the more financially stable member doesn't realize is that the beggar is a veteran of war and , due to mental illness, can't work, or the beggar is disabled and physically cannot lift a hammer to drive the nail labor for monetary gain, or maybe the beggar does work but it's just not enough to support his family like so many Americans in this nation. I ask you, why should our brothers and sisters suffer? What have they done to deserve this great pain of not knowing if they'll make it to the next day or even the next meal? Yes, I understand there are those who exploit the pain of these poor members, and those who do are as bad, if not worse, than the ulcers who yell at the person down on their luck. But for the ones who truly feel this pain, why are they not helped? If this nation is truly for the people, and all are equal, then why should they have to beg for a few dollars? Why should they be forced to live on the sidewalks and in the alleyways of the cold, dark streets? What have they done to deserve this ill fate? Nothing. Nothing but be born in the wrong place. Politicians try to convince us and trick us, saying they're the problem and we should get rid of the homeless. They do things like put spikes under bridges, removing places to sleep, and placing policies in place to prosecute the beggars, but what does that truly do? It only harms our poor brothers and sisters even more and causes them more unnecessary pain. We must help our fellow Americans, pass laws to provide government funding to low income households, put in place public housing to get these poor people off the streets, and give them a real place to live and warm meals to eat. Help them get back on their feet so that they may become functional members of society. Help and love our brothers and sisters; do not hurt them more than they already are. If we are all truly equal, then why aren't we treated that way? Why are some of us looked at like lessers? No more should we stand by and let our people get kicked and pushed around by the government, who swears it's for our own good. It's not for our own good.

The Modern Day Caste

We are led to believe that we have an open class system, a system of free flowing social mobility, and the thought alone of this tends to keep people at bay. But the truth is that we are long barred off from rising the social and economic ladder in America, Louisiana in particular. We're told that hard work and determination leads to social growth, and while in some cases this is true, the overwhelming majority either hardly advance or don't at all. If your father is, or was, a laborer, then, more than likely, so was his father and his before him, and this holds true in most any profession. Of course, there are exceptions to this case with the lucky few that somehow manage to climb up and grab those brass rings of success, but these are far and few between. The figure heads of our nation feed us sensational news topics while behind the scenes they attack our educational and financial well being in an extreme effort to keep us down in the pits that we try ever so hard to climb out of. An example of this here in Louisiana was when former governor Bobby Jindal led a ruthless attack on Louisiana education where he proposed to cut about 80 percent of Louisiana's higher education budget, a budget cut that lead to LSU alone having to cut hundreds of employees. The claims of politicians like Mr. Jindal include sayings like, "Americans should pay for their own education", and it's not that I don't agree, but it's the fact that they can't. The poverty rate in Louisiana sits near twenty percent, the minimum wage sits right at the federal level of $7.25 an hour, and a requirement for a livable wage that most families can't seem to make holds strong in our state. How can the average Louisiana citizen send themselves or their children to a university? A family of three in louisiana needs around fifty thousand dollars a year to survive happily, the graduation rate in louisiana high schools is 78 percent, well below the nations average, and the college graduation rate is only about 35 percent, so tell me, how can we afford to send our children to college if only three quarters of us graduated high school, only about a third of them went to college, and only about a third of that group finished it? Our public school systems needs a revamping to increase education levels and graduation rates, and we need financial help to be able to move our families to that next step. Without this help, we will forever be stuck in a modern day caste system disguised as a free flowing social stratification system. We must stand together to fight the oppression being placed on us by the politicians who only wish to line their pockets and earn one more term.

True equals

Our nation currently stands divided on more issues than one, and these divisions stop all forward progress. The mainstream media tells us that one side or another is wrong and evil and convinces us to constantly be at each other's throats, but I say no more. We must stop the constant fighting with our brothers and sisters in liberty and break down the source of these pains. Black and white men alike must stand together, along with our equal sisters, to shape a nation that truly benefits its people and treats all who inhabit it as equals not only in speech, but also in practice in every way. Tear down the walls of discrimination and focus the anger not on your brothers, but on the overlords of democracy who keep us in chains and force us against each other like some sort of animal in a cage forced to fight. We allow these detrimental circumstances

unwittingly, so now I bring them to your attention. Take a

moment to release your neighbors throat, take a step back,

and look at what the government is doing right beneath our

noses; stay involved not only at the local government

scale, but also the federal. The only way to take power is to

insert ourselves into the conversation and force the giants

of industry to treat us as true equals.

Unionize

A nation by the people is no longer for them and, arguably,

never truly was. We scrape and scrounge every single day

of our lives, while the government officials and corporation

leaders have polygamist affairs with each other in the name

of democracy and a free market, while, in reality, it's really

a politician buying his votes and the corporate figure

making sure his unlawful acts go unnoticed. And who's to

suffer through this unholy bond? The people this nation so

proudly claims to love and support. We're cheated on by

our endearing spouse in the name of one more term and

answered with a blank apology saying it'll never happen

again, but it always does. They throw decoys in our faces

to distract us from the atrocities they lay at our feet in an

attempt to sweep them under the rug. The working man is

starving but is told he is fine and should work harder to get ahead, but he's working as hard as he can, putting in fifty plus hours a week but still hardly has enough to scrape by. He has almost none to support his family, let alone enough to send his children onto better things, meaning they're destined to the same fate as him. He's expected to work until he dies, and even then it's not enough. The politicians in DC push the retirement age further and further back in a desperate attempt to keep every bit of money the working man puts in and claim it's due to longer life expectancy, but what does it matter to a roofer, plumber, or carpenter if he lives until 100 if his body stopped working at fifty five, and he's already had more surgery and broken bones than one can count? We need to band together and unionize to abolish this modern day serfdom. Union dues are only a small fee to pay to fight the oppression of these immoral leaders. With unionization comes the first step to a truly free nation; with it comes a truly livable wage, health insurance, and job security, along with many more necessities as soon as you join. This is the one true way to fight the economic Titans. Stand together with your

brothers and sisters arm in arm and demand your rights,

because together we hold the power of the nation.

Worked to death

The retirement age is at a constant increase. I'm speaking not only in terms of social security and other retirement funds increasing their age requirement without penalty, but also the cost of living. It's gotten to the point where you have to remain in the workforce until about the age of seventy, and this is fine in jobs where little to no physical requirement is needed, such as a government job or office job, but for the working man, this just isn't possible. In a world of work where at the age of 40 it's highly possible and plausible that you've had a numerous amount of surgerys and are plagued with pains every day, how can you be expected to work another 30 years? It's truly inhumane, and these laws get passed because, not only do these people in office not know the true pain of a blue collar job, they simply do not care. They want workers to work until they're dead so no money has to come out of there their pockets to feed the people. The current state of living, any household making less than $40,000 a year cannot comfortably live, and, sadly, this is what many Americans are forced to live with, and it's simply unfair. Why should a man born into riches be more valued than a man who's worked his whole life to support his family, and why is the former what we base our system off of when the working man is the majority? America is no longer a nation for the people and this is merely one example of how that holds true. We must raise the wages of the working man and woman and decrease the cost of living, along with the age of retirement in order to live longer, healthier lives. Think not only of yourself, if this doesn't apply to you, but also your brothers and sisters who must suffer every day of existence.

Your side

It amazes me how little can get done in a single day in DC.

Watching a senator speak behind the podium, basing

actions on their every word is what we expect our

representatives to do, but in reality not a single one has a

seat in the house, because they've already made a decision

based on who pays them more. This seems to be a trickle

down system, where the public divides itself into two major

parties and dance around meaningless arguments, where

there holds no true passion or urgency to make a change,

only arguing to argue and only doing so because they

identify with an ass or an elephant. Well, I'm telling you,

the only ass is the one who sees issues and either doesn't

care or doesn't take action. The two party system that our

country runs on is doing more harm than good, dividing the

nation and political scene, causing a never ending stalemate

where nothing will ever be done, and we grip onto every

word and eat it up with a smile, but why? Why do we listen

to them, why don't we stand up, why don't we take back

what is rightfully ours? We're told this is a nation for the people, but is it really? It sure doesn't feel like it. We should abolish the two party system and run off of an independent platform where anyone and everyone has a chance to be heard, taking the voice from the multi billion dollar corporations and giving it back to us, the people.

Empowerment

We hold no power in the system we live within today. A system that claims to be ran by us is simply controlled by puppets, the master being the almighty dollar that comes from our lords of corporation. We are starved in the name of their prosperity, we are killed in the name of their conquest, and we fight to fuel their power with nothing coming in return. We do not live our lives for us, we live it for them. They own us, and we must break free. It starts locally, stand arm and arm with your brother and do not let them get pushed around. They will do the same for you, then infiltrate their coveted positions, if federal system is something ungraspable for you, then aim towards the local with a small office, make the changes we need. Do not blindly vote, instead inform yourself and your neighbor, but do not indulge in lies just because they suit you, you must accept truth, even if it so pains you to do so. Do not rely on the corporate cow. Instead form your own resources, bring power to the local farmer who ever so struggles with his bills to pay. Shop from the stores run by your equals, not the ones that mass produce world wide. Do unto them as they have done unto us, starve them. Make them beg for forgiveness, then, when they do, deny it, for it will only happen again. We must shape this nation in the true image of the people, in a truly free state that one can prosper.

Dangers of a domestic force

At one time in our nation's history, foreign terror was at the peek of concerns and a sense of unity was needed in order to survive. Well, I challenge you to realize that the same is taking place today, the only difference being it is now our own tyrannical government who we must fear. As they fought unnecessary taxation and under representation, we face a government that sells us off to the corporations and attempts to eliminate our rights. In an attempt to swallow any blackened gold that they can find, our nation is willing to kill any one of us without a second thought and claim it to be for freedom. If it for freedom, then why are we not free? Why is it our lives that must be wasted to fuel their habits and desires? Why must our sons and daughters, brothers and sisters, and neighbors and friends be the ones who die while they sit on their thrones atop their ivory towers, laughing at us labeling us idiots? I say to hell with the endless state of slavery we must endor in the name of justice. There is no justice here. We are a nation of chains, but these shackles will hold me no more. Do not let them

hold you, brother.

Why must we starve.

Education funding takes up six percent of the average national funding, healthcare another six, energy and environment only three, social security, unemployment, and labor in total only three percent, our military budget takes up fifty four percent of the national yearly funding. And why, why must that be? The next most a country spends on military only a third of our budget, after them hardly a tenth. While we conquer the world as nations before us did, now on the search for oil with a mask titled freedom and independence, our people starve, our people cannot afford food, we cannot afford schooling. We cannot afford to live, but thats okay as long as our owners get to line their pockets. We only enter war for material gains and, when there's none to be had, we leave. But when there is, when there is, we kill like no one has ever seen, but it's okay because we put titles on the people we kill to dehumanize them. It's okay, because we're saving the people of the country we've terrorized, it's okay, because we did it for our nation, but what is it our nation's done for

us? It's starved us, it's made it where we cannot afford an

education in order to keep us oppressed, it's given us a

false sense of security and prosperity, while in reality it

robs us blind and leaves us for dead. Why must we starve.

A call for help.

Today there are children homeless across this nation we call home, there are mothers who cannot support their babies, there are people, - innocent people,- who starve and have to wonder when their next meal will be. There are people who are oppressed by their brothers and sisters, there are those who ashamed to be within their own skin. There are fathers who are ashamed in themselves, because they cannot bring home enough to raise the family they've started no matter how hard they try. Today, across our nation, there are politicians who claim to fight for the people but sell them off when given the chance. Today there are businessmen who preach fair wages but undercut the uninformed worker. Today there is suffering and injustice in the world, today there is suffering and injustice in our nation, and today there is suffering and injustice in our hearts. We know we've been cheated, we know we've experienced hate, we know we are not united, yet we do nothing. We must do something. We must stand up to end the pain and suffering, we must stop the hate and focus on a common goal, and we must not fight with ourselves and ignore the true threats. We must do something. Do something.

We are a nation of chains.

A nation of chains, we stand bound to the locks of an economic and political system that slowly kills all not within the powerful elite. We toil over matters of conservative or liberal, and whether we will vote democratic or republican. We worry ourselves with ignorant things such as racism, sexism, and other atrocities that have no place in our society and ignore the lack of payment for our labor. We fight and race for better pay, but we don't slow down to realize we can work together to all be payed a livable wage. We fight over how much we need a job, but we don't realize without us there would be no job. We are the workforce, we are the masses, we are this nation, not some old man in a suit running his multi billion dollar business from the comfort of his office building. We are the farmers, the teachers, the construction workers, we are the single mothers and poor families. We are the people, and we are the nation. We are powerful, but ill informed. We listen to every word that is spoken from the media and the politicians and take it for gospel truth. We do no research of our own, we do not care about the truth, only what we want to hear. I'm telling you, that's not how you should live; be informed, become educated and fight for a better future not only for yourself, but the generations after you. Make an impact on history that cannot be erased. Start a movement, or simply take part in one. Help this nation become one for the people and not for the corporation. We are a nation of chains, enslaved by the corporate and political powers, and they hide the secret that they belong to us. We fear losing a job or wages but, without us, there are no wages for them. We must put in place laws to internalize all national workforces that way they must rely on us for their income, causing us to hold power once more. We must fight for people of our own to take office so we will be treated equally, we must

fight to break up the corporate powers, and we must

make America a place for the working man once again.

Thank you for reading, I hope you are more informed and have gathered opinions of your own, do not take everything I say as facts but instead use what I say to build a framework for your ideology and gather your own information to make yourself enlightened. Thank you for your time and support.

Roy